# FOREWORD

# JUSTICE DELAYED IS JUSTICE DENIED

Most lawyers would agree that many cases should and could be settled on the front end, but it's rarely done. Despite the fact that 95% of all cases settle, most cases settle "on the court house steps" after years of needless and expensive litigation. Why? There is little benefit to either side spending unnecessary time or expense, so how do we break the vicious cycle of litigation?

"Justice delayed is justice denied" is a well known adage in the law. It is hard to know who gets credit for the oft quoted maxim, but surely we all get the blame. The failure to attribute the quote only shows that people throughout history were plagued with time stealing from them a sense of justice.

In 1970, former Chief Justice Warren Burger warned that one of the great threats to the American people's belief in justice would be inefficiency and delay stealing it from them. In an age of technology where people expect faster results, that problem is now. When I began practicing in 1992, things were different. There were no emails in 1992, so "snail mail" ruled the day. The justice system moved as slow as the mail, but in a society used to snail mail, the slower pace of justice was understood. Faxed pleadings were "revolutionary" then but are now a waste of paper and time. Today, everyone uses email. Emailed pleadings and communications are the norm. As society moves faster, people and clients expect litigation to move faster, for "justice delayed is justice denied."

As technology progressed, so has the need to speed up the resolution of cases and address the problem of "justice delayed is justice denied." It's no surprise that the idea of resolving cases earlier via mediation was born in the 1990s just as technology was taking root. Getting people to accept mediation was not easy. There was a time when courts weren't sure of it, when clients and attorneys weren't sure if they trusted it. People were fearful of participating and "playing their hand" prior to going to court. They weren't sure if what they said at mediation could be used against them later. Now, mediation is the norm. The change has taken root. People expect it. Court's often require it. Many states and courts establish certification requirements for mediators and passed or promulgated the necessary laws and procedures to order it and enforce its processes. Mediation is firmly imbedded into our system.

Few would argue, though, that mediation solved the problem of "justice delayed is justice denied." It often comes too late or after too much expense. It's a tool, but not an end in and of itself.

The idea of "early case resolution" is but one imperfect idea to address the problem of a fair, early resolution. It allows a representative of a company to reach out and directly negotiate a disputed claim with plaintiff's counsel, quickly, without any need for an intermediary and typical formal discovery.

Early resolution is a tool to combat the problem of "justice delayed is justice denied." The purpose of this short book is to impart some of the lessons I learned from two years of doing early resolution within Walmart tort litigation, and those lessons are: (1) how to institutionalize early resolution as a process within a litigation department, either within a large insurance defense firm to deliver better value for clients or within the large institutional clients big enough to have such programs; (2) share negotiations lessons learned for individuals negotiating early resolution of the claims.

# TABLE OF CONTENTS

Time for Change ............................................. 7

Litigation Doesn't Deter Litigation ..........................9

Corporations Control Your Dockets ........................15

The Role of OC in ERT .......................................... 21

What Skill Sets are Required for ERT Members? ..................... 22

The Dedicated Early Resolution Counsel ........................ 23

The Art of Negotiation – the Judo ROLL ....................... 25

    Relationship ........................................................27

    Practice Pointer: The Negotiator's Reputation ........29

    Objective Fairness ............................................. 29

    Listening ........................................................... 31

    Practice Pointer: Key Points of Listening ................... 33

    Practice Pointer: Effective Listening Behaviors ..........34

    Levers of Negotiation ......................................... 34

    Practice Pointer- Don't say "can't" ............................ 35

The Four Interests in Every Negotiation ........................ 36

What is Settlement Value? ........................................ 36

Determining Settlement Value, Yours and Theirs ................. 37

When do negotiations begin ....................................... 38

**The First Phone Call, Establishing the Relationship** ............... 40

**Specific Negotiation Techniques** ......................................... 41

**The Winds of Change** .................................................................. 44

**About the Author** ........................................................................ 45

## TIME FOR CHANGE

After twenty-one years of practicing law in a small family practice, at almost fifty years of age, I was looking for a change. I went down the street and interviewed with Walmart legal. What happened next was not what I expected. My future boss was looking for a change too.

My future boss had an innovative idea to change the way of traditional litigation in corporate litigation. Most lawyers would agree there are many cases that should and could be settled on the front end, but it's rarely done. Despite everyone agreeing things should be different, they remained the same. The traditional litigation system plodded along. How to change that?

Since 95% or more of all cases settled, my boss wanted to see if cases could be settled on the front as opposed the back end after incurring so much time and expense. Could they be settled earlier as opposed to later and settled at a fair value? He asked me to use my experience, my common sense, to find cases and see if early resolution could work.

I liked the idea, but where would I begin? How would I insert myself into a case without creating problems for our outside counsel? What would I say to plaintiff's counsel? How would I explain who I was and what I was doing without it appearing we were capitulating? Would plaintiff's counsel embrace this new idea that things should be different? How, as an employee with the company, could I discuss the merits of a case without my conversations being a "statement against interest" made by a party-opponent? There were more questions than answers.

In my first twelve months, I personally settled 260 personal injury cases, ranging from simple slip and falls, to truck accidents, to product claims. Those settlements included three wrongful death suits on three different issues on three different types of cases, one involving an infant.

I learned that early resolution can work, but the program unfortunately died when my boss left for a new position and his replacement didn't continue it, and we went back to the model of litigating to settle.  So, although early resolution can work, the most important lesson was to make it fundamental; it has to become part of a company's processes and attorneys need to focus on negotiation and not chest thumping.

## LITIGATION DOESN'T DETER LITIGATION

Common sense says if litigation deterred litigation it would have gone the way of the horse and buggy long ago, but litigation is alive and well and despite generations of tough litigation it is growing. My own experience with Walmart proved this to be true. Long before I arrived at Walmart, they had a reputation for tough litigation, but despite that tough reputation, it didn't deter litigation against them. Litigation hasn't proven itself a deterrent and if anything, has proven it increases it. Be wary of whoever argues litigation is a deterrent and ask what they do for a living. I also have to wonder, if litigation is such a deterrent, why do almost all cases settle? The truth is, aren't litigating cases, we are settling them.

Does early resolution encourage litigation? No. After two years of doing nothing but early resolution, it didn't increase the amount of litigation against Walmart.

There is growing recognition that traditional litigation isn't working to deter litigation or get a fairer result for either side – it's too time consuming and expensive, and despite the banter of "seeing you in court", 95% of all cases settle. So, why not settle 95% of the cases sooner rather than later?

The need for early case resolution arises from the limitations of the traditional litigation model which isn't designed to allow early resolution. In the traditional litigation model, a corporate defendant is sued and assigns defense of that suit to outside counsel. In a typical slip and fall case, the defense counsel will then do a physical store visit, interview employees, take depositions of the plaintiff and the plaintiff's experts and witnesses, and after the expenditure of great time and effort, will recommend to the defendant that it settle, on average, 95% of the time. But this recommendation usually only comes after extensive, expensive, litigation.

In the traditional system, plaintiff's counsel often feels the need to "work" the case to influence defense counsel's risk assessment and eventual settlement recommendation. This means plaintiff's counsel spends more on experts, depositions, etc. It involves a great deal of posturing between counsels. Defense counsel is never at a point to recommend settlement early because the plaintiff continues to increase "risks" by working their case up and the defense then counters that risk with the addition of experts to deny experts, more witnesses, etc. In this traditional cycle, there's always more discovery to answer, more depositions to be taken. The big losers in this traditional process are the clients, for "justice delayed is justice denied."

Some cases demand the kind of attention given by the traditional litigation model, but many do not. Not all cases require the tremendous expenditure of time and resources to recommend settlement, and the defendant and plaintiff end up spending more time and money defending and prosecuting lawsuits just to settle them than they would if they settled early.

In the typical litigation model, 95% of all lawsuits settle. Why do 95% of all cases eventually settle after so much pre-trial posturing? Despite the banter of going to trial, trial is risky. The risk is not just born by the individual plaintiff or individual defendant; it presents risk to trial counsels. Keep in mind there are four parties to every settlement: the plaintiff, the defendant, plaintiff's counsel and defense counsel, all of whom have a financial stake in the outcome and despite the pre-trial banter, ultimately seek resolution.

Going to trial puts considerable risk on all four parties, not just the two clients. The plaintiff may get nothing at trial and the defendant may pay a lot at trial, or the verdict may be a mixed result for either, leaving both unhappy. But the attorneys can also lose financially and lose reputation by trying a case. The plaintiff's attorney can lose reputation and lots of money and costs advanced if he either loses or doesn't recover enough at trial. Defense counsel can lose a client if he loses at trial. Thus there is an incentive for all four parties to settle.

The problem with the traditional model is cases typically settle at the time least advantageous for the parties. Both parties' legal costs and risks increase the longer the case takes. Thus, parties incur maximum costs by settling "at the courthouse steps" or even at mediation. Why? Many parties treat mediation as a mini-trial and incur significant the costs and expense preparing for trial prior to mediation.

Why does early settlement work? It works for the same reason most cases settle, because 95% of all cases settle. The only question is when that settlement will happen. All parties have an interest in settling early to avoid unnecessary time, expense and risk. Many plaintiff fee agreements are structured so that the plaintiff pays a reduced attorney fee if a case settles early. Not all cases can be settled with early resolution, but many can. Identify and settle the ones that can and save time and resources for the ones that can't.

Thinking has to change. This traditional system isn't delivering justice, it is delaying it. All parties need to focus on the idea of settling earlier, not later. On the corporate side, it requires implementing process changes which to allow early resolution. One the individual side, it requires individual attorneys and representatives focus on developing requisite "negotiation" skills to allow cases to settle and quit chest thumping.

## CORPORATIONS CONTROL YOUR DOCKETS

In the current system, the corporation puts itself at the mercy of outside counsel. Some outside counsel are better than others, but the problem remains, under the traditional model, corporations rely solely on their OC to investigate and report risk. Why? If nothing else, "time is money" and when a defendant relies solely on outside counsel to assess and try to settle a case, it takes a lot of time and money to get to resolution. The corporation needs to give itself the ability to control "their docket" and resolve cases early when possible freeing outside counsel to try cases if necessary.

To do this the corporation needs to establish an **Early Resolution Team (ERT)**. Why? Despite the well intentioned efforts of individual attorneys, if the corporate governance doesn't set up a process to take hold of its own litigation and focus on resolving cases early, it won't happen. So, if a corporation wants to take charge of its own litigation destiny, it needs to set up a written process establishing an ERT.

The ERT is given the authority under corporate governance to review lawsuits and negotiate those suits to conclusion. The written process will include the parameters of suits which can be reviewed and monetary authority given. For example, will the ERT only review slip and falls? Auto accidents? Surgery cases or non-surgery cases? Product liability cases? There are any number of parameters which can be established for ERT review and resolution.

ERT relies on the justice of speed, the company needs a streamlined process for negotiators to quickly access people within the business to get the authority needed to resolve a claim quickly and without the usual requirement for depositions, formal discovery, etc., which typically accompany formal request for authority.

After the parameters are established for what types of cases should be resolved early, if possible, analytics will produce a spreadsheet for the team to review. This can be daily, weekly, but needs to be produced timely enough that the team can act on it quickly. The spreadsheet includes basic information about the suit, the name and age of the plaintiff and a short summary of the claim from the claims file. Each ERT uses their discretion to identify suits from this spreadsheet for early resolution.

Even with ERT, all suits are sent to outside counsel (OC) for defense. ERT does not stop the usual assignment to OC for defense. Even with ERT, OC will file an answer or other necessary pleadings to protect the defendant's interest. The difference with ERT is, if a suit is identified by ERT for early resolution, the ERT will notify OC via email that the case is identified for early resolution and that the ERT member will take over management of that case and engage in direct negotiations with opposing counsel. OC is instructed to withhold from any work not necessary to protect the right to defend. For example, in a retail case, OC refrains from doing the typical store visit, discovery.

The ERT member simultaneously initiates contact with opposing counsel to begin settlement discussions. Initial contact may be by phone or email. Whether initially by phone or email, opposing counsel is sent a form "settlement discussion" email to insure the communications are protected settlement discussions.

ERTs don't engage in discovery when negotiating a settlement. If plaintiff's counsel insists on production of information, they are asked to submit a formal discovery request to outside counsel. ERT follows the discovery rules to avoid discovery issues should the case not settle about what was or was not produced. Following the formal rules of discovery is a subtle reminder of the value of early settlement, that each side will must work harder if they want to fight over issues. Generally, experience shows that if a suit went through the insurance claims phase first, discovery isn't needed for early resolution.

If a settlement is reached, the ERT member confirms the settlement with opposing counsel and OC drafts the necessary paperwork to finalize the settlement agreement.

If ERT is unable to resolve the case, then ERT transfers control of the file to a normal case handler that then manages OC through conclusion of the case. Some states have offer of judgment statutes with "teeth", meaning if the offer is refused and not exceeded at trial, the opposing party may pay costs, attorneys' fees or both. States which come to mind are California, Colorado and Florida. In states that allow offers of judgment with "teeth", ERT has the option of putting their final offer into an offer of judgment.

Putting a final offer into an offer of judgment allows minimal expenditure of costs on the front end and maximizes the opportunity to recover defense costs and/or expenses if the plaintiff doesn't beat the offer at trial. Some would argue this is a wasted argument that judgments are not recoverable against individual plaintiffs. This isn't always the case. It is rare, but some judgments are recoverable against individual plaintiffs. Sometimes, plaintiffs are advised to take out cheap insurance coverage indemnifying them against an offer of judgment should they lose, still other times the success on an offer of judgment can be used to negotiate away an appeal. At a minimum, an offer of judgment will force the opposing attorney to relay the offer to their client. Though attorneys have an ethical duty to relay offers, there is a surprising number that do not. The offer of judgment seems to correct that problem.

## The Role of OC in ERT

Though OC isn't engaged to do its typical defense workup, it plays an active role in advising and assisting the ERT member with resolution of the case. Some cases require more OC assistance than others. Typically, the OC will insure ERT understands any jurisdictional limits of the court where the case is filed, for many states have courts of limited jurisdiction which also affect what discovery may be had or may have expedited scheduling orders. OC will advise ERT of any special issues concerning the judge, counsel or parties which OC is aware of that ERT is not. OC may be asked for an initial settlement value of the case either based on information in the claims file only or with assumptions known and made by ERT. Sometimes, ERT may require an early mediation and OC participates in that. There are any number of ways OC's role continues to be important in the ERT process.

## What Skill Sets are Required for ERT Members?

Negotiation skills are the main requirement. When selecting individuals to work early case resolution, keep in mind you are picking negotiators. The person you select will not be an attorney defending the suit and will not be an adjuster adjusting a claim. They are a negotiator trying to resolve a claim. That is a different role than most are used to playing.

To be a negotiator on litigated claims, one does needs a solid understanding of the law and civil procedure, but, more importantly, one must be seasoned in direct negotiations. It is more important that the negotiator have good people skills and good emotional intelligence than it is they have a good understanding of the law. Why? Because negotiators can rely on OC to answer specific legal questions when they arise, but the negotiator can't resolve anything without good people skills.

## Dedicated Resolution Counsel Apart from ERT

For optimal effectiveness, the defendant needs a dedicated ERT attorney, one not bound by the parameters established for ERT. What is the difference between the dedicated attorney and ERT? There are two differences. The dedicated ERT is an attorney whereas ERT members don't have to be and the ERT Attorney has no parameters as to which suits to review.

The exercise of common sense and discretion (both of which are the growth of experience) is critical to success. The need for early resolution requires the use of common sense to identify and settle suits which could, or should, be settled. For the system to be a success, it needs common sense discretion to function properly. The experienced ERT attorney is free to peruse any suit and use his/her discretion to try and resolve the suit.

Though parameters for ERT are well intended, policies and procedures often develop rigidity and begin to work opposite the goal of using common sense thus defeating the purpose for which the rules were promulgated. For a company to feel comfortable that it is "protected," it needs a "roving linebacker" working its defense and reporting problems found and trying to solve those problems. A dedicated resolution counsel empowers a company, not just the litigation department, but the company as a whole to respond quickly to unforeseen tragic cases even before the claims stage.

The dedicated resolution counsel needs to be an experienced trial attorney to fully appreciate the nuances of cases that often hinge on intangibles. The experience of trial work, prepping cases for trial, depositions, being in the courtroom, and dealing with opposing counsel and judges is critical experience to develop the "common sense" resolution counsel needs to fully appreciate risks of any particular case, personalities, respect for others, garner respect from others, and present a case for resolution both within the company and without.

The dedicated resolution counsel should report to the head of the litigation department. Why? less bureaucracy equals faster response times. Speed is important to all parties.

## The Art of Negotiation – the Judo ROLL

Why learn negotiation? Negotiation is a life skill, not just a skill for resolving lawsuits. We do it every day with loved ones, friends, at work, with the people we meet. It is a skill that can be learned. If you learn to master the art of negotiation, you learn to master the conflict in your life.

Negotiation is "verbal judo." Judo is the gentle art of rolling your opponent to an advantageous position. Negotiation is the gentle art of using persuasion to roll your opponent to a favorable position. The *Cambridge Dictionaries Online* defines a negotiator as "someone whose job is to try to help two groups who disagree with each other to reach an agreement." That's better, but how does a negotiator get two groups that disagree to agree? The definition is incomplete. It is void of the human emotion which accompanies the "deliberation and discussion," between "two groups who disagree." In practice, negotiation is the **art of persuading** two groups who disagree to agree and the negotiator is a persuader. Persuasion is "The act of influencing the mind by arguments or reasons offered, or by anything that moves the mind or passions, or inclines the will to a determination." *Marx vs. Threet*, 131 Ala. 340, 30 So. 831, *Black's Law Dictionary*, 2nd Ed.

Negotiators need to learn the art of verbal Judo to be effective. The Judo "Roll" is an acronym for: (1) Relationship, (2) Objective Fairness, (3) Listening, and (4) Levers of Negotiation.

Negotiation is a skill that can be learned. If one remembers the Judo ROLL, they will begin to master the art of negotiation.

## Relationship

Establishing a working "relationship" is the heart of the art in reaching a settlement. A positive working relationship allows two parties to negotiate differences of substance. The relationship begins with the first contact and continues to the last contact. It is a constant process. To establish and maintain an "effective" negotiating relationship, every contact must be "soft on the person, firm on the problem." Every contact should convey honesty, fairness, and respect. Never say, write or do anything you will regret. Assume everything you say, do or write is recorded and will be played back to the judge, jury or on the evening news. There is truth to the idea of negotiation Karma that you get what you give. If you are fair, they will be fair. If you are reasonable, they will be reasonable. If you listen, they listen. Yelling and anger are disrespectful, and beget yelling and disrespect.

Studies show that approximately 60% of all communication is non-verbal, 30% is tone, and 10% the words we use. In ERT negotiations the percentages change. ERT negotiations are typically over the phone, so tone of voice is 90% of communication.

Small talk is important to relationship. There is a saying that "small talk gets big results." All studies show that small talk helps solidify a working "relationship" by establishing rapport with your opponent. Do not force small talk, but take the opportunity to engage when it is presented – it always is. For example, if your opponent says, "I'm sorry I didn't get back with you sooner I was out on vacation," take the opportunity to ask, "Where did you go?"

## Practice Pointer: The negotiator's reputation

Reputation is either a shadow covering you in suspicion or a warm light inviting discussion. To be successful, a negotiator needs a reputation for honesty and fairness in every negotiation. There are times when an opposing party is none of these things, but even in those situations, if a negotiator maintains his/her reputation via effective communication, honesty and fairness, while showing respect, a good negotiator can reach a good settlement despite a non-reciprocal opposing counsel.

## Objective Fairness

Fairness requires special emphasis. Emotional influences are important to human decision making. We are all familiar with the "fight or flight" syndrome. Negotiations are the same. If your opponent perceives your offers as "unfair" aka arbitrary, it will literally incite a physical response to "fight" you meaning argue with you. This is why all actions must project fairness. If not, the negotiation is likely to fail. Fairness includes respect for the other party, the art of listening and the use of objective criteria to value claims and not being arbitrary, in the offers you make.

Avoid your opponent's "fight" response by being fair. How? If your opponent knows the basis for your offer there's a better chance is will be considered "fair," even if they don't agree with it. If considered fair, they will negotiate with you and not argue with you.

For example, don't simply offer $5,000.00 for an injury. Always take the time to explain "I've considered the $1,500 in medical bills. I understand she has $500 in lost wages, and I'm adding to that for her claim of pain and suffering putting a value on this claim of $5,000.00). An offer without explanation is deemed arbitrary and unfair.

You will see later how objective fairness and "levers of negotiation" are the same. Fairness means that when you begin negotiating using your negotiation levers, you always speak in the common language of liability or damages when presenting offers.

## Listening

Always listen! Never miss a good opportunity to be quiet! As the Dalai Lama said "When you talk, you are only repeating what you already know. But if you listen, you may learn something new." Do not go into a settlement discussion talking. Do not begin a negotiation with the false assumption you understand either liability or damages. If you do, you will not listen. The other side always has information you don't have. Find out what that information is. Find out the strengths and weaknesses of their case. Ask lots of open ended questions. If they know you sincerely listen, they talk to you. What they tell you may either change your risk analysis or concede facts that hurt their case and can be used as negotiation levers by you.

The negotiator understands a demand is an offer to compromise. People often get upset by threatening oral demands or letters. Negotiators don't. Strongly worded statements or letters are intended to influence the emotions of the person receiving it, but in the end, it is an offer to compromise. A demand is a **temporary** positional statement of a party; it is a means to a perceived settlement value based on known facts and current temporal interests of the parties at the time it is made. Strong emotional wording or threats in a demand are a negotiation tactic. Remember, negotiation is all about human decision making. The negotiator's job is to move through that positional statement and uncover the opposing party's settlement position.

Demands go up or down over time. They are always temporary because the needs of the four parties constantly change. Risks differ with each individual and differ for each individual at any point in time. The risk to the plaintiff and the risk to their attorney are different. One may need money now for bills unrelated to the claim, whereas the other may not. So, needs are based on time, and time is a "risk" factor. Each individual in a negotiation has different needs, different risk tolerances.

A demand says a lot about the person and claim, by either what is said or not said. If a demand has a deadline, timing is important. How can this be used by you to resolve the claim? If the demand gives a "take it or leave it" number, find out why and how was this figure was derived? The take it or leave it number gives important clues as to the interest of both the attorney and their client making the demand.

### Practice Pointer: Key Points of Listening

1. Effective listening satisfies the other side's emotional interest to be heard and then, they will be able to listen to you;
2. You can listen without agreeing;

3. Gain useful information (knowledge is power).

## Practice Pointer: Effective Listening Behaviors

1. Paraphrase what they said without agreeing. This insures you have understood;
2. Inquire with open ended questions. Illicit what you don't know;
3. Acknowledge their feelings, their tone, to demonstrate your understanding.

## Levers for Negotiation

After one has established a relationship, listened and understands the other side and the facts of their case, then they can begin the negotiation. Always speak with respect and in the language of negotiation, meaning the common language of litigation. In litigation, the common language of liability is the jury instruction on liability, what is the law? Is it a pure comparative state? Contributory negligence state? The common language of damages is speaking in terms of what that state allows and what the evidence shows. What is the standard for punitive? What do the facts show?

## Practice Pointer- Don't Say Can't

Can't is a negative. It implies you don't have authority. Crisis negotiators never tell a hostage taker "we can't." No matter how crazy the demand, they don't say, "can't." For example, if someone holding hostages says, "I want a plane and $10 million dollars in an hour," the hostage negotiator won't say, "I can't." They will say, "I need more time," or "I need you to do this for me."

You must convey you are the right person to talk to and that, with the right evidence, the negotiator can resolve the case. If the negotiator says, "I can't," that implies they aren't the right person. "I've got all the authority you need if you get me the right evidence."

## The Four Interests in Every Negotiation

To understand the art of settling a case, one must understand the financial motivations of all parties in settling. The four parties are the plaintiff, the plaintiff's attorney, the defendant, and defense counsel. All parties eventually settle for the same reason – money earned or saved. The Plaintiff wants to recover money; plaintiff's counsel wants to make money and recover the costs and expenses advanced or not incur them; defense counsel makes money by defending and maintaining a future relationship with the client, and the defendant wants to save money, by paying as little as possible, with recognition it will have to pay something even if it's the cost of defense.

## What is Settlement Value?

The settlement value is the dollar value of the case that exceeds the risk of going to trial at any point in time in the evolution of a case. It is almost always fluid, as it is based on current costs, known risks and interests of the parties. It is temporal. It creates opportunities for compromise on all sides.

## Determining Settlement Value, Yours and Theirs

Initial settlement value takes into consideration both the "costs" and "risk" of trial. "Costs" includes financial cost of the litigation (attorney fees, expenses, and expert costs), cost to company/party reputation, cost of a parties time away from work, the emotional cost to the party (family cases, death cases), the risk of prolonged litigation on the party (interest accruing on medical bills, risk of collection, risk of loss of evidence, etc). Beyond the "costs" of going to trial, the "risk" of trial is the risk of attaining a particular jury verdict in a particular venue. How good is the liability and what are average verdicts in this county for this type of case? There are many jury verdict research tools that assist with this calculation. In more serious cases, one would consider OC's experience on these types of cases in this venue and in front of this judge.

An initial settlement value is derived before negotiating, but this isn't a final value for settlement purposes. A final settlement value isn't reached until after discussing the case with opposing counsel to insure all the facts and risks are understood. Opposing counsel may disclose a fact which changes the evaluation for better or for worse.

## When do Negotiations begin?

Negotiation begins with the first contact with opposing counsel, whether that contact is the first pleading, email, phone call, etc. Every communication is a step towards eventual resolution.

Generally, negotiations are initiated with a "demand" from a plaintiff but can be initiated with an "offer" from the defendant. In either case, one should insure the demand or offer is protected by Rule of Evidence 408 by including the language of Rule 408 in their demand or offer.

Below is a sample form offer from the ERT. The intent of this email is to provide a process for confidential settlement discussions to take place, provide a framework for those discussions (time/manner/parties involved), establish a relationship with opposing counsel by introducing the negotiator, the negotiator's intent, role, and relationship to outside counsel, a time table for resolving the case which introduces risk and parameters, and a brief discussion of substance without argument (showing an openness to discuss), and makes an initial offer to show fairness if enough information is available to do so. Keep in mind that all offers must written with the belief that plaintiff's counsel will share them with their clients as they are supposed to do. The offer should be written in a way that conveys your sincerity, as if you were sitting in a mediation speaking to the plaintiff.

## The First Phone Call
## Establishing a Relationship

The first phone call will not settle the claim, but will establish a relationship to do so. The "tone" of this first phone call sets the tone for all future discussions. If this phone call doesn't go well, you may kill the ability to settle the claim at a later date. A positive phone call will hopefully open the door of opportunity to resolve the case by getting your opponent out of the "fight" mode of litigation and into the "settlement" mode necessary for resolution. Tone of voice is the way they will "see" you and judge you. First impressions are lasting impressions.

Keep the call simple. Identify yourself, confirm they received your email, and reiterate your intent to resolve the claim. Listen often. Talk little. Learn as much as possible.

## Specific Negotiation Techniques

**Person to Person Contact** – Experience shows person to person contact is needed to settle a case. This is typically done with phone calls.

**Tone of voice** – Tone of voice is critical to settlement – it must be a tone which conveys you want to settle the case if possible. At all times, be polite and courteous. If they call you "sir" or "Ma'am" reciprocate. Do not be overly formal, for a relaxed tone is conducive to getting them to relax and negotiate as opposed to posture.

**Don't argue** – As a general rule, don't argue the case. Arguing is "personal." It is not "listening," and it is not a discussion of substantive issues of liability or damages. There is a difference between substantive discussions of facts and arguing. When the other side argues, listen and acknowledge. Attorneys often want to argue their strong points on liability or damages. Arguing is them attempting to insert risk. Don't take the bait. Deflect arguments pointing out that liability is never certain and is always a risk for both sides. Deflect arguments on damages with substantive questions on damages. Damage evaluations on either side are always wrought with uncertainties leaving room for substantive questions.

**Early Fair Offer of Settlement** – Plaintiff's often put a high arbitrary value on their initial demand to insert risk to the defendant or because they believe the defendant will increase their reserves on a case. Likewise, defendants often put too low a value on a claim to entice a plaintiff to engage in negotiations. Both sides are being arbitrary, unfair and reap what they sow. Your first offer must be fair to initiate a meaningful reply. A fair offer typically begets a fair reply.

**Never lie** – Don't lie about anything. If you lose the trust you lose the ability to settle and you affect you reputation forever. Be truthful.

**Time** – Time is a critical. **Always have enough time to talk and never feel pressured to compromise.** If you are rushed in a conversation, you risk damaging the relationship. If you are rushed for time, you get hurried and make concessions or get angry which will hurt a negotiation. So, if you have limited time for a call, let the other side know what that time limit is, for example, begin by saying "Is this a good time for you?" or if they call you are limited, let them know "I only have fifteen minutes and if that's not enough, let's schedule a time now to get back in touch." Time is also a motivator for all sides to settle. Mediators often use the trial date and costs of trial to insert risk. The ERT negotiator can do the same.

**Patience** – A negotiator needs patience, patience to listen, patience to wait, patience not to respond negatively.

## THE WINDS OF CHANGE

Just as there was a need for mediation to speed resolution in a system too slow to deliver timely justice, there is a growing need for common sense resolution earlier than what formal mediation provides. Early resolution is the topic of the day. There is recognition of the need but little experience to develop programs to implement it. Early resolution must overcome the same hurdles faced by mediation in its infancy, gaining trust of all participants. It requires setting up processes and people qualified to do it. My experience with early resolution is positive. I hope these thoughts add to the discussion of allowing common sense resolution without unnecessary litigation on cases that deserve it.

# About the Author

Chris Lisle received his law degree from the University of Arkansas in 1993 and began practicing law with his Father. He has over Twenty years' trial experience handling complex litigation including construction defects, personal injury, criminal, contracts, real estate, and other matters and along the way created a bit of new law in the following reported decisions:

*Mears v. Nationwide Mut. Ins. Co.*, 91 F.3d 1118 (C.A.8, Ark., 1996); *Shepherd v. Washington County*, 331 Ark 480, 962 SW 2d 779 (1998) Case of First Impression interpreting Arkansas Civil Rights Act; *Bedford v. Fox*, 333 Ark 509, 970 SW 2d 251 (1998) Case of First Impression under Arkansas Usury law; *Arkansas Democrat Gazette v. Zimmerman*, 341 Ark 771 (2000), Writ of Certiorari holding court's gag order was an abuse of discretion; *Brown v. Johnson*, 81 Ark App 60, 90 SW 30 924 (2003); Holding that an adopted child was excluded from a deed; *Mobley Law Firm P.A. v. Lisle Law Firm P.A.*, 353 Ark 828, 120 SW 3d 537 (2003), Holding client had "cause" for terminating attorney's services; *Benton County Stone, Inc. vs. Benton County Planning Board*, 374 Ark 519, 288 S.W.3d 653 (2008), decision upholding the denial of a re-zoning request.

After his father passed, he began doing early resolution for Walmart. He's attended Harvard's basic negotiation course and "Difficult Conversations" course.

He is a veteran of the US Army, having served in the 82nd Airborne Division. He completed Army Ranger School (awarded Ranger Tab, 1989); Army Parachute School, and German Parachute Wings. He enlisted after high school, was later commissioned in college, and honorably discharged as a Captain in the Infantry (USAR). He completed an Iron Distance Triathlon, Four Marathons, climbed Mt. Kilimanjaro in Africa, and has made fire without matches.

www.ingramcontent.com/pod-product-compliance
Lightning Source LLC
Chambersburg PA
CBHW030057230526
45471CB00003B/1133